I0055138

Jeff Bowick & Dwayne Henriksen

OPTIONS TRADING CRASH COURSE: INVESTING FOR BEGINNERS

Learn how to operate in the market in the best way even if you are just a beginner

© **Copyright 2021 - All rights reserved.**

This document is geared towards providing exact and reliable information in regard to the topic and issue covered.

- From a Declaration of Principles which was accepted and approved equally by a Committee of the American Bar Association and a Committee of Publishers and Associations.

In no way is it legal to reproduce, duplicate, or transmit any part of this document in either electronic means or in printed format. All rights reserved.

The information provided herein is stated to be truthful and consistent, in that any liability, in terms of inattention or otherwise, by any usage or abuse of any policies, processes, or directions contained within is the solitary and utter responsibility of the recipient reader. Under no circumstances will any legal responsibility or blame be held against the publisher for any reparation, damages, or monetary loss due to the information herein, either directly or indirectly.

Respective authors own all copyrights not held by the publisher.

The information herein is offered for informational purposes solely and is universal as so. The presentation of the information is without contract or any type of guarantee assurance.

The trademarks that are used are without any consent, and the publication of the trademark is without permission or backing by the trademark owner. All trademarks and brands within this book are for clarifying purposes only and are owned by the owners themselves, not affiliated with this document.

Table of Contents

INTRODUCTION

Options trading can be daunting for those with little to no experience, but it doesn't have to be.

What are Options?

You can buy a stock outright, you can short sell stocks and you could even trade options. There is a buyer and a seller for every option and the seller is obligated to fulfill the contract should the buyer choose to exercise it.

If you're using options as a way to trade stocks, a put option is basically insurance against losing money. If you own stocks and fear they might drop in value, you can buy put option contracts to protect the stocks from losing too much. If the stocks don't drop, you don't have to do anything else and your put option expires worthless. That way you avoid losing money on your original investment. If you're looking to trade options as an investment strategy on its own, then buying call option contracts is a good way to do it. If you think a stock is going to go up in value, you can buy call options contracts with a strike price that's higher than the current market price. That way you can make money if the stock goes up. If the stock doesn't go up, your option expires worthless and you lose the money that you paid for it. Your goal in that situation would be to buy the stocks at the strike price and then sell them for a higher price.

Types of Options

There are two main types of options: equity and index.

Equity options are the rights to buy a specific stock at a specific price in the future. Index options are rights to buy or sell an entire index, like the S&P 500.

These are known as futures options but they work in similar ways to equity and index options.

You can also trade options on currency pairs. Instead of buying the US dollar or any other currency, you can buy options on the exchange rate between two currencies. In this case, the underlying asset is currencies and not stocks.

Using Options in Your Portfolio

One of the great things about options trading is that it lets you take a more active role in your portfolio. If you have stocks that are performing poorly but that you think still have the potential to go up, you can buy put option contracts to protect your investment. This way you don't have to sell your stocks and take a loss, giving them a second chance to go up in value. Buying put option contracts is also a great way to hedge your portfolio. If you have stocks that are doing well but you're afraid that they might have a correction, you can buy put option contracts to protect your portfolio. If the stocks don't drop in value, you don't have to do anything and your put option contracts expire worthlessly. If your stocks do drop in value, the put option contracts allow you to sell your stocks at the predetermined price and then buy them back with the option contract. This way you can avoid losing money on your original investment.

You can also use options to trade stocks. Whatever you decide to do with them, having a solid understanding of options trading will help you make the right decision for yourself.

CHAPTER 1   ANALYZE THE MARKET

You are not psychic. It is impossible to accurately predict the outcome of your stock to the last detail. However, you can become near perfect at reading the stock market by learning how to analyze this market's components properly. There are two basic types of analyses: technical analysis and fundamental analysis.

Fundamental Market Analysis

Fundamental analysis involves getting data about a company's stocks or a particular sector in the stock market, via financial records, company assets, economic reports, and market share. Analysts and investors can conduct fundamental analysis via the metrics on a corporation's financial statement. These metrics include cash flow statements, balance sheet statements, footnotes, and income statements. Most times, you can get a company's financial statement through a 10-k report in the database. In addition to this, the SEC's EDGAR is an excellent place to get the financial statement of the company you are interested in. With the financial statement, you can deduce the revenues, expenses, and profits a company has made.

For example, the quick ratio and current ratio are useful in determining if a company will pay its short-term liabilities with the current asset. If the current ratio is less than 1, the company is in poor financial health and may not recover from its short-term debt. Here's another example: a stock analyst can use the debt ratio to measure the company's current level of debt. If the debt ratio is above 1, it means the company has more debt than assets, and it's only a matter of time before it goes under.

Technical Market Analysis

This is the second part of the stock market analysis, and it revolves around studying past market actions to predict the stock price direction. Technical analysts put more focus on the price and volume of shares. Additionally, they analyze the market as a whole and study the supply and demand factors that dictate market movement. In technical analyses, charts are of inestimable value. Charts are a vital tool as they show the graphical representation of a stock's trend within a set time frame. What's more? Technical investors can identify and mark specific areas as resistance or support levels on a chart. The resistance level is a previous high stock price before the current price.

On the other hand, support levels are represented by a previous low before the current stock price. Therefore, a break below the support levels marks the beginning of a bearish trend. Alternatively, a break above the resistance level marks the beginning of a bullish market trend. Technical analysis is only useful when the rise and fall of stock prices are influenced by supply and demand forces. However, technical analysis is mostly rendered ineffective in the face of outside forces that affect stock prices such as stock splits, dividend announcements, scandals, changes in management, mergers, and so on.

Stock Market Corrections and Crash

A stock market crash is every investor's nightmare. It is usually challenging to watch stocks that you've spent so many years accumulating diminish before your very eyes. Yes, this is how volatile the stock market is. Stock market crashes usually include a very sudden and sharp drop in stock prices, and it might herald the beginning of a bear market. On the other hand, stock market corrections occur when the market drops by 10 percent - this is just the market's way of balancing itself. The current bull market has gone through 5 market corrections.

Why You Need to Diversify

According to research by Ned Davis, a bear market occurs every 3.5 years and has an average lifespan of 15 months. One thing is exact, though: you can't avoid bear markets. You can, however, avoid the risks that come with investing in a single investment portfolio. Let's look at a common mistake that new investors typically make. Research points to the fact that individual stocks dwindle to a loss of 100 percent. By throwing in your lot with one company, you are exposing yourself to many setbacks. For example, you can lose your money if a corporation is embroiled in a scandal, poor leadership, and regulatory issues. So, how can you balance out your losses? By investing in the index as mentioned earlier, fund or ETF fund, as these indexes hold many different stocks, as by doing this, you've automatically diversified your investment. Here's a nugget to cherish: put 90 percent of your investment funds in an index fund, and put the remaining 10 percent in an individual stock that you trust.

When to Sell Your Stocks

One thing is sure - you are not going to hold your stocks forever. All our investment advice and energies are directed towards buying. Yes, it is the buying of stocks that kick-start the entire investment when chasing your dream concept. However, just as every beginning has an end, you will eventually sell every stock you buy. It is the natural order. Even so, selling off stock is not an easy decision. Heck! It's even harder to determine the right time to sell. This is the point where greed and human emotions start to battle with pragmatism. Many investors try to make sensible selling decisions solely based on price movements. However, this is not a sure strategy, as it is still sensible to hold onto a stock that has fallen in value.

Conversely, selling a stock when it has reached your target is seen as prudent. So, how can you navigate around this dilemma?

Why Selling Is So Hard

Do you know why it's so hard to let go of your stocks even when you have a fixed strategy to follow? The answer lies in human greed. When making decisions, it's an innate human tendency to be greedy. Here's an example: An investor purchases shares at $30 and tells herself that she will sell when the stocks hit $40. Here comes an all-too-familiar trend - when the stocks finally hit $40, the investor will hold out and see if her stock prices will rise beyond $40. You can see that human nature is already creeping in. Undoubtedly, the stocks hit $45, and greed takes over logical thinking. She decides to wait to see if it rises beyond $45. Suddenly, the stock prices plummet down to $36. She tells herself that once the stocks rise again to $40, she will sell. Unfortunately, this never happens. This stock continues to plummet down to $25. Finally, she succumbs to her frustrations and sells at $25.

Greed and irrationality took over her sound investment plan. In this scenario, sound investment plans were replaced with gambling tendencies. Although the investment was a loss at $5 per share, her actual loss stands at $20 per share. This is because she had the opportunity to sell at $45, but she held out, hoping for even higher prices. Knowing when to sell is truly a paramount factor. Sometimes, the right selling decision that brings some profits to your table might look like a poor selling decision. However, in this scenario, it's advised to say prudent. To remove human emotions from your decisions, you can consider adding a limit order that automatically locks your selling decision. The limit order will sell once it reaches your target price.

Is The Company Suffering from Any Setback?

These days we have access to a lot more information than we ever had. As you have continued access to the internet, it can be challenging not to check market data continually. However, beware that doing this can make you succumb to emotional triggers, which might ultimately lead to poor selling decisions. Compare the company's total revenues to its benchmark and others in the same sector. This can help you discern if the slow performance indicates falling stock prices or just a random market movement.

Is Your Portfolio Out of Balance?

As an ideal investor, you have diversified your investment across various sectors. Over time, some stocks begin to perform better than others in that portfolio, making your investments shift towards the out-performers. Therefore, it is necessary to bring your investments back in line to conform to your fixed asset plan. In this situation, you are faced with two options to even the scales: you either buy more of the stocks that have fallen behind or sell the outperforming stocks.

Will You Get a Tax Break?

Yes, your investments have reached your target price, and you can wait to sell. Before you do, remember that selling a stock that has increased in a tax-prone brokerage account can trigger a tax bill. The rate of the tax depends on whether you have held the investment for more than a year. If you have, you are eligible for a reduced long-term capital tax rate. If not, you will attract higher short-term tax rates.

Is There a Better Investment for Your Money?

According to billionaire investor and guru, Warren Buffet, the best holding time is forever. However, that's pretty unrealistic for an investor with a finite income. Sometimes, we sell off investments to meet individual needs such as retirement, college funds, vacations, and anything else that requires capital. Admittedly, it's wise to sell off stocks to meet up with current cash needs and avoid the volatility of the market. However, I advise not to use your long-term funds for your immediate needs.

How Will You Make Your Exit?

Once again, you are not psychic. It is nearly impossible to time a perfect sale - you don't know when a stock is at its lowest point or when it's at its highest point. Running to sell off your stocks can save you from losing more, and it also denies you the opportunity to gain additional income if the stock rises. Those are the uncertainties that you have to deal with as an investor. However, there's a trick to selling your shares. You can sell shares at different periods. If you sell them all at once, you might lose out on additional opportunities. If the stock has good potential, you should sell part of it and hold on to the rest.

CHAPTER 2 MAKE A
WINNING PLAN

One of the most important ingredients in any investment plan is a winning, long-term strategy that understands the market and is intended to give you an edge over other investors.

It's a formula that can't be created, to some extent, by anyone. It has to be carefully formulated by a skilled practitioner who understands the basics of investing and market conditions.

If your investment plan is based on a winning strategy, you're more likely to get returns that beat the market averages and provide a lifetime income stream for your heirs.

Your plan may also help you avoid investors with poor money management skills and thus avoid costly mistakes that can result in serious loss of capital.

That's what wins.

"Major Market Investor" is the title of a book written by financial expert Dr. Doug Duncan (formerly a staff economist for the Federal Reserve Bank of New York). The book is filled with practical advice on how to develop a winning investment plan and apply that plan to successful investing in the stock market.

Duncan's commitment to providing students and investors with practical strategies to help them achieve their investment objectives makes him one of the most knowledgeable and successful educators in the field today.

I'm not going to assume that you know anything about economics, finance or investments. Nor am I going to suggest that you simply subscribe to one of the many Wall Street advice books or magazines out there.

You also need a specific plan with priorities in place so your money gets invested properly at each stage of your life.

Once you have a winning long-term strategy, it's important to have a plan for managing that strategy. You need to know how much risk you are willing to take, and how you are going to handle the inevitable drawdown when markets go down. This is where planning, budgeting and daily discipline come into play.

You must understand the markets

The most successful investors I know all understand the markets very well. Those who understand less tend to make more mistakes, especially when markets are trending or in a roller-coaster ride.

Instead, they base their investment decisions on economics and fundamentals – despite the fact that these aren't always easy to read. A strategy built upon these foundations will produce better results than one based on technical analysis alone.

The fundamentals of the market are quite simple. The more people who want to buy a stock or bond, the higher its price will become, and vice versa. This is very basic, but it's not always easy to see. The reason for that is that there is also a psychological aspect that tends to push prices even further away from their fundamentals.

So if you want to be successful in investing without any help from others, you have to cut through this psychological layer of the market and learn to read its numbers and ratios. This is exactly what the fundamental indicators do. They help you distinguish between the various factors that drive stock and bond prices, and help you build a strategy that will give you a decisive advantage over others.

How to use fundamental indicators

Fundamental indicators are quite easy to understand: they are the numbers and ratios that reveal the underlying economic fundamentals of a company or security. For example, take the case of Intercontinental Exchange (NYSE: ICE), a US-based company with operations in North America, Europe and Asia. Its fundamentals include revenue, profit (both net and gross), assets, liabilities, and so on.

Then check the EPS numbers against industry averages to see if it's performing well.

Keep in mind that what we care about is a company's earnings growth more than its price growth. The price will follow the earnings, so if you spot a company with strong growth in its fundamentals you'll have reason to be optimistic and willing to invest.

On the other hand, if the fundamentals are weak or deteriorating it may be best to avoid that company, even if its stock is trading at a bargain.

You can take this analysis further by examining how each fundamental indicator is performing compared to its own historical levels. For example, if a company's inventory has continuously grown over the last few quarters, then you should investigate whether the management is doing anything to improve its efficiency.

A simple ratio analysis can be very useful in spotting these kinds of problems. You can find out the historical growth rate of a company's sales, or its EPS, and compare that with what's happening now. If there is a big difference between them, you may have found an area of concern that you should investigate further.

The stock market is all about risk and reward.

Some recommendations are:

-Know what kind of investments you want to make (stock, bonds, or other).

-Maintain a diverse portfolio so that when one investment has a down year, at least some of your money will be doing well in others.

-Cultivate the habit of regular saving and investing.

-Decide what is a reasonable investment horizon for yourself and stick to it.

-Invest in an index fund, such as the well-known S&P 500 index of large cap stocks.

-Do not try to time the market. As in other things, it is far easier to be almost right than just right. It is much better to buy too early than too late, but don't try to predict the exact market top or bottom either way . . .

-Do not try to time the market. As in other things, it is far easier to be almost right than just right. It is much better to buy too early than too late, but don't try to predict the exact market top or bottom either way...

-If you decide that you need some money and cannot get it from your own savings, see if your company can match or contribute part of it.

CHAPTER 3 PROTECT YOUR PORTFOLIO

Learn how to protect your investment with these 10 tips.

Tip #1: Invest in mutual funds that have been around the longest.

When you invest in a mutual fund, you are buying shares of a company's stock or other security. Mutual funds are simply groups of stocks with pooled money and are managed by an investment manager who attempts to make a profit for the fund's shareholders. When looking for the best mutual funds, finding those that have been around the longest is your best bet.

According to this website, the longer a fund has been in existence, the more time it has had to develop its winning strategy and improve its performance. In addition, it has had time to attract investors and build awareness of itself as a worthwhile investment option. The longer a fund has been in existence, the more likely it is to have a strong track record.

Tip #2: Use primarily exchange-traded funds (ETFs) in your portfolio.

Exchange-traded funds (ETFs) are an alternative to traditional mutual funds that share their investment objective with mutual funds. First, ETFs are usually cheaper than traditional mutual funds.

Index Funds are another alternative to traditional mutual funds that are very similar. In fact, many Index Funds are simply mutual funds that follow the makeup of an index. The main difference is that traditional mutual funds have an active manager who makes the decisions on which stocks and/or securities to buy and sell while an Index Fund simply buys the stocks within a specific index based on its makeup.

Tip #3: Use low-fee funds whenever possible.

Examine the expense ratios of your mutual fund(s) to make sure they are low enough for you to profit from future returns without paying excessive fees.

You can find the expense ratios of each mutual fund you are interested in by visiting the website for the investment company or fund manager.. Also, some mutual fund companies offer classes of shares with different expense ratios so you will want to pay attention to these additional features when choosing your investments.

Tip #4: Do not invest in actively-managed funds.

Passively managed funds are the exact opposite of actively-managed funds and are, therefore, your best bet when looking to choose the best mutual fund. With an actively-managed fund, a portfolio manager is making decisions on which stocks and/or securities to buy and sell within the fund based on his or her knowledge and opinions. With a passively-managed fund, the portfolio manager is not making any decisions and simply does not buy or sell securities within the fund.

Tip #5: Go with an index mutual fund for a passive management approach.

As mentioned above, if you are seeking to invest in a mutual fund that has low fees but still offers some diversity in its holdings, you should consider an index mutual fund as your best bet.

Index mutual funds primarily follow an index, which is simply the makeup of stocks or other securities within a specific industry sector. Index mutual funds essentially hold all the stocks within a specific index and are therefore better options for those who are looking for low fees and some diversity in their holdings.

Tip #6: Select funds that have low turnover rates.

This often means that a mutual fund pays an investment advisory firm to trade the fund's shares on its behalf. While this may save the mutual fund company money, you can expect to pay for this arrangement through higher fees. To determine if a mutual fund has high turnover or not, look at its turnover ratio. This is calculated by taking the cost of sales (which is found in a mutual fund's annual report) and dividing it by average net assets (which is also found in its annual report).

Tip #7: Read the fund's performance.

Reading a mutual fund's annual report should be your first step when choosing a mutual fund. This report usually includes information on the performance of the fund in the 12 months preceding its filing date. Examine this information to make sure it matches up to what you are looking for in an investment. A strong prior year performance, especially when compared to its peers, can be considered a good sign as well as a signal that there may be room for improvement or even growth within the future.

Tip #8: Ask questions.

The best way to ensure you receive the attention you need when choosing a mutual fund is to ask questions. It's important that you are satisfied with your final decision and feel confident that it is doing what can be expected of it.

To ask questions, first make sure you have chosen the best mutual fund based on the tips above. Then, contact your investment advisor(s), who will be able to help you choose the right mutual funds for your specific needs and goals. If you don't feel as though you are satisfied after speaking with your advisor, ask him or her to refer you to someone else.

Tip #9: Consider a "fund of funds."

If you are looking for additional diversity when compared to an index fund, consider an investment which combines multiple index funds into one investment. This is known as a "fund of funds. " A fund of funds provides access to multiple mutual funds, including the one you have held. This allows you to potentially benefit from the higher returns that may come with actively-managed funds while still taking advantage of low fees incurred by index fund holdings.

Tip #10: Know when to invest and when not to.

Mutual funds are an ideal way for many people to grow their money over time, as long as they are invested in a low-cost option. However, it can be risky to depend on mutual funds alone. If your investments have been stagnant for a long period of time (especially if they have been in mutual funds for a while), you may want to consider other options such as stocks or real estate. Investments which do not change within an established pattern and supply you with additional income are far less risky than investing in an index fund or most other types of mutual funds.

Bump up quality instead of quantity by focusing on these 10 tips. Follow these tips when choosing a mutual fund and you will be well on your way to a safe, rewarding investment!

CHAPTER 4 HOW TO REDUCE RISK INCREASING PROFIT?

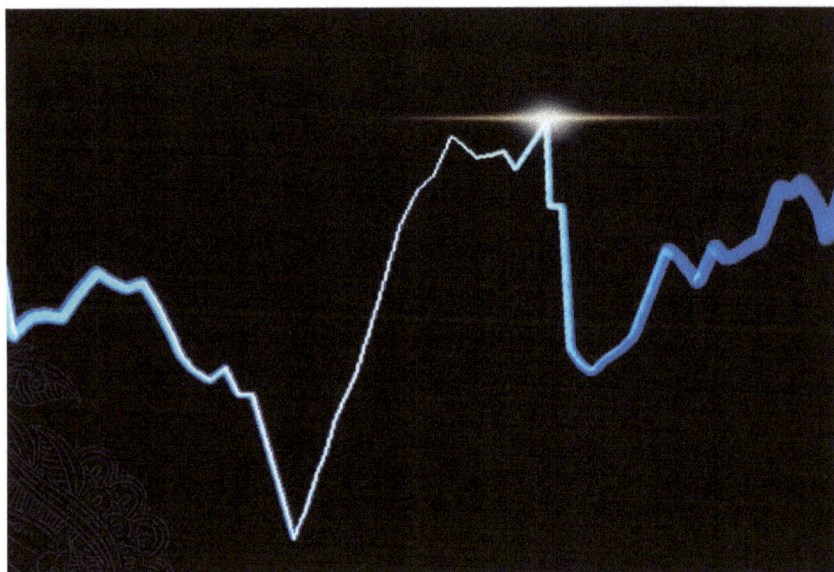

Making money is about taking risks and investing in the stock market has become one of the most common ways to make a profit. If you invest in stocks, you might notice that your account balance begins to increase over time as your investment grows. The problem with this is that it can easily lead investors into a false sense of security. In order to avoid this effect, you must first analyze the risk and reward of different stocks before buying them.

You can analyze the potential risks associated with stock investments by using the appropriate sources of information. The following are the sources of information that you need to consider when choosing stocks:

The first source of information is a company's recent financial reports. You should get a copy of the latest income statement, balance sheet and cash flow statement for each company that you plan to invest in. This will help you identify several issues, such as:

a. The company's financial position (in terms of assets, liabilities and equity)

b. The financial position of the company compared to those of its competitors

c. The company's future prospects and growth potential

d. Historical trends for the business

You want to invest in the stock market, but at the same time, don't want to lose too much money if things go wrong. How can you ensure your investments are less risky?

The key point is that you must invest in the right stocks. It's important to study the market and choose stocks with as high a profit margin as possible, particularly if you aren't experienced and have not yet developed a good understanding of how stock investing works.

Let's examine each of the three basic types of risk that investors face:

– Loss Risk- This refers to the losses that arise from declining performance or default on their obligations. The first type of loss is when the company's operations are not as promising as they seemed before. Sometimes they will make a large investment that does not pay off and they lose money. The second type of loss is when the company fails to meet its financial obligations, which can include paying off debts or paying dividends to their investors.

Due to these issues, you want to invest in companies that don't carry much risk due to increasing profits. In other words, stocks that have a high profit margin. With this you can minimize your loss risk and even turn it into a potential profit.

– Liquidity Risk- This refers to the difficulties investors face when trying to sell stocks quickly for cash or other assets. Stocks that are easily tradable on the market offer higher liquidity compared to those which take longer to sell.

In order to reduce this risk, you should invest in stocks that have a low market share and high liquidity.

– Volatility Risk- This refers to the volatility of stock prices. Volatility risk is an important issue for small investors, as they are more likely to be affected by these fluctuations in the market.

In order to reduce the risk over time, market volatility is also a key consideration. For this reason, you should invest in stocks that have a low market share and low volatility.

Reducing risk involves identifying the company's financial position compared to those of its competitors, as well as calculating their potential future profits. You should also take into consideration the future prospects of the company and historical trends to identify any major changes that may occur in the stock price.

If you want to reduce your risk, then avoid stocks that are too volatile. The stocks with low volatility offer a safer investment compared to those with high volatility as you can use this information to forecast the potential movement of stock prices in the future.

In addition, you can reduce risk by investing in those stocks that have a high profit margin. This is because the stocks with a higher profit margin will give the investor the highest returns in return for higher risk. In addition, you can also increase your profits even further if you invest in such companies which have a very low market share and high market liquidity.

So there is little difference between paying more or earning more than others for the same risks that investors face in stocks.

One way is by diversifying their investments. If you diversify your investments, then you will be distributing your risk. For example, if a company in your portfolio does poorly, but the rest of the market is doing well, then you won't lose as much money.

This is why mutual funds are so popular for investors who want to reduce their risk.

So how do investors diversify their investments? One popular way is by using exchange traded funds (ETFs). ETFs are essentially mutual funds that trade on a stock exchange like stocks do. This gives investors the ease of trading stocks, but without the brokerage commission fees.

Another popular way to reduce risk when investing in the stock market is through indexing. Indexing is what allows you to invest in an entire market instead of just stocks. Instead of investing in specific companies, you can invest in the entire market through mutual funds and ETFs that track the market.

Any time you want to invest in individual stocks, you want to make sure that you do your due diligence first. Do research on the company and know what makes a good company before investing.

Any time you invest in stocks, it's important that you use stop loss orders. A stop loss order will sell your stocks if they fall below a certain price. That way, you won't lose any money if things don't go as planned.

Another way to reduce risk when investing is by making sure that your stocks are covered in case anything happens to you. This is why many investors buy life insurance so that their families will be taken care of if something happens to them.

If you stick to these tips, then you can invest in the stock market with less risk. Remember that the more research you do on a company, the better off you'll be. And don't forget about stop loss orders - they could save you a ton of money.

CHAPTER 5 TIPS TO GET STARTED

#1 Stay informed about your investments: read company reports, annual reports, management presentations and keep up with news from analysts.

#2 Start with a conservative portfolio: if you are starting from scratch, invest relatively conservatively. Get an objective view of your risk profile and target portfolio exposure to minimize volatility.

#3 Don't get emotionally involved: avoid having any emotional attachment to your investments. As Warren Buffett puts it: "Only when the tide goes out do you discover who's been swimming naked."

#4 Stick to index funds: there is no easy way getting started in investing. A good place to start is index funds. There are many different types of index funds but the most popular type is the S&P 500 index. Even if you cannot afford to invest in the top 500 companies, it can be a very good place to start.

#5 Start with a target date fund: these funds track the stock market and provide a certain level of protection against unintended investment losses. Target date funds are intended to achieve higher returns than most in the market and will only move into riskier investments once they approach their growth in retirement.

#6 Use an adviser or an automated platform: there is no easy way to get started in investing but if you have not yet considered hiring an adviser, consider using a third party automated platform today. Compared to a traditional portfolio, automated platforms are able to provide a level of risk controlling that can be hard for humans to achieve.

#7 Get informed about taxes: the primary goal is to earn more income from your investments. The taxes paid on your investments will depend on two things: how much you invest and the types of investments you invest in. If you make good choices, tax planning is important but it can be annoying when you do not understand how these changes might affect your portfolio returns.

#8 Create regular saving habits: if you can only save once a month, try to do it. It is easier to reach your goals if you are able to save regularly. Saving in an account that pays a fixed return is the way to go.

#9 Pay off credit card debt: if possible, pay off your highest interest credit card debt first. It is easy to forget about paying off your credit card debt when you have other pressing financial demands, but it is a good idea to start paying it off as soon as possible.

#10 Don't give up: if one of the first 10 tips does not appeal to you, just give it another try. It takes time and effort before you can get into the habit of investing regularly. Once you do, it feels like you are back in college again and learning new things every day.

#11 Stay focused: the day to day life of an investor is a constant struggle against emotional and behavioral barriers.

Staying focused on your long term goals will help you keep the right perspective.

CHAPTER 6 11 TIPS TO MINIMIZE RISKS AND MAXIMIZE PROFIT

1. Risk is inherent to investing.

2. In order to make money, you must take some risk in your investment decisions.

3. But it doesn't mean that you should invest everything that you have into a single company or asset class.

4. You can reduce the amount of risk by diversifying your investments, which means spreading them out among several different investment choices and asset classes (stocks, bonds, real estate).

5. Diversifying your investment portfolio means investing in a mix of asset classes and companies.

6. In a nutshell, diversifying means that you should invest in:

- various asset classes like stocks certificates of deposit, money markets, bonds, short-term real estate and other financial instruments

- different industries like telecommunications, finance, manufacturing or technology for example

7. Diversifying your investments means that you should have a variety of different types of investments.

8. Make sure to diversify based on your personal circumstances, like your age, tax bracket, risk tolerance and liquidity needs (ability to sell quickly).

9. Stay diversified no matter what happens with one company or asset class. Stick with the investment plan you have in place – don't change it every time the market goes down or up.

10. If you are worried that the value of your investments is going down, don't sell too soon.

11. If you lose money investing in stocks, don't blame yourself; it's not always your fault.

CHAPTER 7 11 TIPS TO HAVE THE RIGHT MINDSET

1. Investing is about risk and return

2. You can only make money when everything breaks in your favor

3. In the short term, you will ALWAYS lose some money while investing

4. The amount of money you have invested should not be a determining factor of success or failure

5. If the worst happens and you lose all your investments, it's a learning experience

6. Focus on long term benefits rather than short-term gains or losses

7. Prepare 5 years of living expenses in advance for emergencies

8. Don't just have one pillar of investment

9. Have a plan B and plan C

10. Only invest if you fully understand the product or service

11. You will always lose money in investing, be ready to take the hit, then continue to learn from your loss and move on with your life.

CHAPTER 8 11 TIPS TO USE IF YOUR PORTFOLIO IS GETTING DOWN

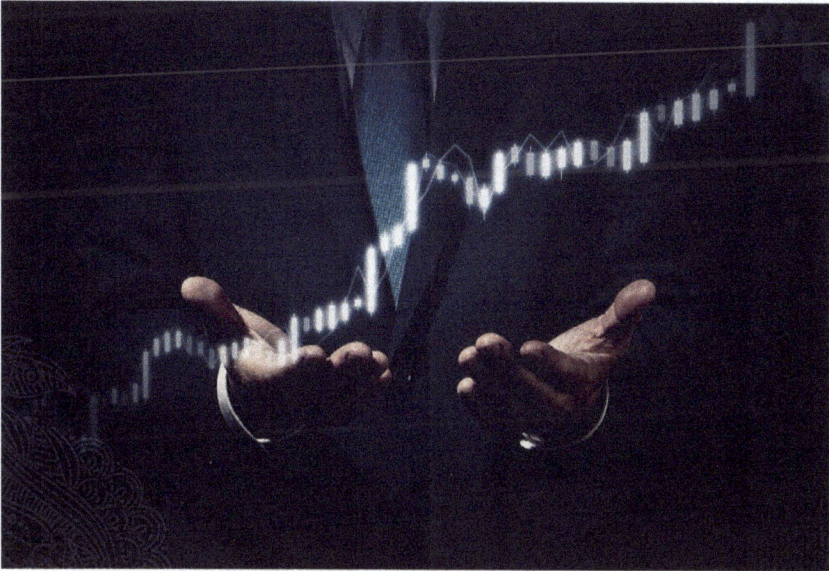

1- Keep your website updated. Keep adding new artworks, so that people always have something new to see and enjoy.

2- Have a social media account for your work. Twitter and Instagram are the most common ones! It's simple to advertise your work through these social media sites as they're easy to use and not overly expensive for their services.

3- Strategy on where and how you're going to sell your artworks. It's not always because of the notoriety that people will buy your work, it can also be because they like the work itself.

4- Don't try to over saturate one website or social media account. This can result in your piece being lost in the mire of other artworks or just being ignored completely.

5- Don't put all of your eggs in one basket. Although there's no point in having multiple artworks on sites such as Etsy,

6- Don't be ashamed if you don't sell any pieces. Even if things don't go well, it doesn't mean that you're a failure. It just means that you need to try a bit harder!

7- Having trouble selling anything? I suggest checking out the tips for selling from the artists site - The Artists Network. If they're not selling any pieces and they have some tips, then you should definitely take a read.

8- Make sure that your online portfolio is good enough to make people want to buy something. If you can't convince someone to buy your work, then you can't sell anything.

9- Find a couple of sites where your work could be included and ask for permission. If you're not keen on letting other artists use your artworks, then it's better to ask for permission. But of course, if you can't think of any artists that would be good to ask, no worries! As long as your work is good enough, it shouldn't matter who uses it as long as a decent price is paid.

10- Don't stop trying in the end, it's only you who is going to get your work sold.

11- Don't give up! It's the enemy of success and there's no doubt that if you keep trying, you'll succeed.

CHAPTER 9 HOW TO
MAXIMIZE PROFITS

Monitoring the Trend

Trends are a graphical measure of the actual activities that are taking place in the day trading market.

Any trader closely following up the trend makes him or her informed and accurate in his or her levels of predictions and chances are that winning may be their middle name. They are able to purchase when the prices are high and short sell when they drop. Analyzing trends has several assumptions in that, if there are continuous cases of rising prices, possibilities are that they will constantly happen and vice versa.

News on Trading

News always comes in two ways; good news and bad news. Well, good news on day trading always gives the traders and brokers a huge motivation to purchase prices at good rates. When it comes to bad news, on the other hand, the traders are given an opportunity to short sell prices. This kind of strategy can be used as a great move in making huge amounts of profits at a particular season and induce high volatility rates.

Scalping

Scalping takes advantage of the small kind of prices that happen drastically during the day trading sessions. This kind of mechanism involves getting engaged so quickly and so fast and then leaving right away.

Contrarian Investing

This kind of strategy describes the assumption that prices will go up and most probably reverse and then drop. The contrarian buys during fall or short sell during the rise periods. The attitude in this kind of strategy defines that the whole expectation idea is to subdue to change and that things are to head in a reverse kind of direction.

Financial Management

Capital is so lucrative in any kind of income-generating activity. There is always going to be several wins and losses. Not to sound so risky, most of the traders will not input 2% of their capital in any line of trade. Be careful in whatever you consider as an investment; money loss is ever an option too.

Also, there may be cases where brokers demand high rates of commissions, do not fall into that trap. That is going to cause you big time. Consider the rates of commissions demanded by brokers in the first place because too many expenses in commissions can definitely incur low rates of profits basically meaning that losses will be incurred.

Proper Time Management

Day trading is a journey. A certain market trading journey, meaning that for it to be called a journey, a particular process is established. A certain planned time span is encouraged. Monitor everyday trading move that occurs and will occur for it makes you learn and experience all about day trading. Good things take time, mastering the day trading occurrences is quite an investment. Remember those good investments imply good rates of profits.

Consistency/ Stability

Another point to add, day trading is quite logical. Day trading cannot be analyzed by fear or even greed. Mathematical approaches have to be considered. Set strategies have to be put in place too! Examine every logical operation bound to happen during day trading so as to possess certain clear stability. Once stability has been established, expect some big-time profit rates and an excellent reputation.

Timing

The trading market becomes volatile every single trading day. Experienced traders have mastered the moves and so they are quite sure about what steps to take once they get to read the structures. As a beginner, do not be quite in a rush to predict. Take one or more time to examine every single trend and get your desired prediction. Do not be too slow though, you may end missing so much.

Momentum

This kind of strategy defines revolving around new sources and also identifying the substantial trending moves at high stake. You basically should basically maintain your current position, be alert with the reversing signs and face a totally different direction.

Strong Focus on One Particular Market

Many traders become overexcited and want to trade with all markets. This should not be the case; you will end up being confused not knowing which trade to focus on. It is normally healthy for the business when you decide and focus on one trade, be good at it. Focusing on many trades at a go will make you lose.

Trading Pivots

Trading pivots come in when you buy low at the end of the day and you sell at the high end of the trading day. Once you get to master these tactics, chances are that you will be an expert in comprehending the volatility of the market and therefore declare yourself successful using this kind.

Risk Control

For beginners, it is highly recommended that they engage in trading infrequently as a way of avoiding too many risks. The essence of this is to help them master their moves and learn a lot. Day trading is not just about profits only; it is about taking each day as a learning trading progress. Predict the trends at least after some minutes and not just seconds. I am familiar with the adage that declares that, commit many mistakes to learn highly, but honey, this is some real cash being retrieved from your pocket; you can become poor any minute. Slow but sure steps are highly recommended. Take each trading day as a lesson. With this, tricks and knowledge are so equipped and with no time you will be so okay.

Passive Position Management

A novice day trader is prone to adjust their target and stops abruptly because of being controlled by certain emotions. These kinds of emotions are caused by the sudden updates of the figures and trends on the screen that keep changing with time. This is so confusing for the beginners and, after all causing them to alter their predictions hence leading to a great downfall. Only highly experienced and confident day traders can analyze the updates because they may actually know what they are doing.

For the novice day traders, leave the targets and the stops on their own, and learn how you would passively control all these. Reach for some paper material and sketch and assume how the aftermath would be without interfering with your active trends. Do some in-depth examination and comprehend why every move is happening. In the end, compare what you would have affected your trading account if at all you altered the last trends. This is a learning process. Do this for quite a while and within no time, day trading becomes your all-time income-generating hobby. Yes!

Protect Your Capital

Losses are normally involved in almost all businesses despite that try your best and protect the capital of your business. This can be achieved by shunning from all unnecessary risks that come along in businesses. This will definitely bring success to your business.

Risk reward ratio of 3:1

Comprehending the proper 3:1 risk-reward ratio is so important. This kind of ratio reward encourages a trader to lose small and then win big despite the frequent times you lost on the trading platform. The moment you gain some wide experience, the risk-reward ratio gets higher and higher, meaning that you are slowly advancing and enjoying some good profits. This is the kind of measure we need to strategize to grow as traders.

Patience and Persistence

Plan your trades before you trade your plans. This kind of strategy defines the behavior where most traders do not really trade daily. They have this kind of paradoxical behavior where they just check up on the trends without necessarily acting up because of the fear of outlining the wrong prediction. Well, this is not really a way of learning. Day trading calls for patience and persistence where several wrongs did are part of the journey and learning happens a lot through that. Carefully plan your trades and then predict, see how this goes. Be patient and persistent in every move you make. After all, good things always take time.

Hard Work

Day trading requires you to be hard working to be successful. It is not like the entertainment business which you can joke around with. It needs maximum practices into trading and discipline. You have to be trading frequently and stay updated on the stock price fluctuations.

The above strategies help to improve time factors, skills, financial management operations, to grow as a person, risk management and most importantly, you get to learn.

CHAPTER 10 RISK MANAGEMENT

Excellent risk management can save the worst trading strategy, but horrible risk management will sink even the best strategy. This is a lesson that many traders learn painfully over time, and I suggest you learn this by heart and install it deep within you even if you can't fully comprehend that statement.

Risk management has many different elements to both quantitative and qualitative. When it comes to options trading, the quantitative side is minimal thanks to the nature of options limiting risk by themselves. However, the qualitative side deserves much attention.

Risk

What is risk at any rate? Logically, it is the probability of you losing all of your money. In trading terms, you can think of it as being the probability of your actions, putting you on a path to losing all of your capital. An excellent way to think about the need for proper risk management is to ask yourself what a lousy trader would do. Forget trading, what would a lousy business person do with their capital?

Well, they would spend it on useless stuff that adds nothing to the bottom line. They would also increase expenses, market poorly, not take care of their employees, and be undisciplined with regards to their processes. While trading, you don't have employees or marketing needs, so you don't need to worry about that.

Do you have suppliers and costs? Well, yes, you do. Your supplier is your broker, and you pay fees to execute your trades. That is the cost of access. In directional trading, you have high costs as well because taking losses is a necessary part of trading. With market neutral or non-directional trading, your losses are going to be minimal, but you should still seek to minimize them.

What about discipline? Do you think you can trade and analyze the market thoroughly if you've just returned home from your job and are tired? If you didn't sleep properly last night, or if you've argued with your spouse or partner? The point I'm making is that the more you behave like a terrible business owner, the more you increase your risk of failure.

Odds and Averages

Trading requires you to think a bit differently about profitability. I spoke about minimizing costs, and your first thought must have been to seek to reduce losses and maximize wins. This is a natural product of linear or ordered thinking. The market, however, is chaotic, and linear thinking is going to get you nowhere.

Instead, you must think about averages and odds. Averages imply that you need to worry about your average loss size and your average win size. Seek to decrease the former and increase the latter. Notice that when we talk about averages, we're not necessarily talking about reducing the total number of losses. You can reduce the average by either reducing the sum of your losses or by increasing the number of losing trades while keeping the sum of the losses constant. This is a shift in thinking you must make.

Thinking in this way sets you up nicely to think in terms of odds because, in chaotic systems, all you can bank on are odds playing out in the long run. For example, if you flip a coin, do you know in advance whether it's going to be heads or tails? Probably not. But if someone asked you to predict the distribution of heads versus tails over 10,000 flips, you could reasonably guess that it'll be 5000 heads and 5000 tails. You might be off by a few flips either way, but you'll be pretty close percentage-wise.

The greater the number of flips, the lesser your error percentage will be. This is because the odds inherent in a pattern that occurs in a chaotic system express themselves best over the long run. Your trading strategy is precisely such a pattern. The market is a chaotic system. Hence, you should focus on executing your strategy as it is meant to be executed over and over again and worry about profitability only in the long run.

Contrast this with the usual attitude of traders who seek to win every single trade. This is impossible to accomplish since no trading strategy or pattern is correct 100% of the time.

This is because you don't have to do much when trading options. You enter and then monitor the trade. Sure, it helps to have some directional bias, but even if you get it wrong, your losses will be extremely limited, and you're more likely to hit winners than losers.

Despite this, always think of your strategy in terms of its odds. There are two basic metrics to measure this. The first is the win rate of your system. This is simply the percentage of winners you have. The second is your payout ratio, which is the average win size divided by the average loss size.

Together, these two metrics will determine how profitable your system is. Both of them play off one another, and a decrease in another usually meets an increase in one. It takes an extremely skillful trader to increase both simultaneously.

Risk per Trade

The quantitative side of risk management when it comes to options trading is lesser than what you need to take care of when trading directionally. However, this doesn't mean there's nothing to worry about. Perhaps your risk per trade is the most significant metric of them all. The risk per trade is what ultimately governs your profitability.

How much should you risk per trade? Common wisdom says that you should restrict this to 2% of your capital. For options trading purposes, this is perfectly fine. Once you build your skill and can see opportunities better, I'd suggest increasing it to a higher level.

A point that you must understand here is that you must keep your risk per trade consistent for it to have any effect. You might see an excellent setup and think that it has no chance of failure, but the truth is that you don't know how things will turn out. Even the prettiest setup has every chance of failing, and the ugliest setup you can think of may result in a profit. So never adjust your position size based on how something looks.

Calculating your position size for a trade is a pretty straightforward task. Every option's strategy will have a fixed maximum risk amount. Divide the capital risk by this amount, and that gives you your position size. Round the position size down to the whole number since you can only buy whole number lots when it comes to contract sizes.

For example, let's say your maximum risk is $50 per lot on the trade. Your capital is $10,000. Your risk per trade is 2%. So, the amount you're risking on that trade is 2% of 10,000, which is $200. Divide this by 50, and you get 4. Hence, your position size is four contracts or 400 shares. (You'll buy the contracts, not the shares.)

Why is it important to keep your risk per trade consistent? Well, recall that your average win and loss size is important when it comes to determining your profitability. These, in conjunction with your strategy's success rate, determine how much money you'll make. If you keep shifting your risk amount per trade, you'll shift your win and loss sizes. You might argue that since it's an average, you can always adjust amounts to reflect an average.

My counter to that is, how would you know which trades to adjust in advance? You won't know which ones are going to be a win or a loss, so you won't know which trade sizes to adjust to meet the average. Hence, keep it consistent across all trades and let the math work for you.

Aside from risk per trade, there are some simple metrics you should keep track of as part of your quantitative risk management plan.

Drawdown

A drawdown refers to the reduction in capital your account experiences. Drawdowns by themselves always occur. The metrics you should be measuring are the maximum drawdown and recovery period. If you think of your account's balance as a curve, the maximum drawdown is the biggest peak to trough distance in dollars. The recovery period is the subsequent time it took for your account to make new equity high.

If your risk per trade is far too high, your max drawdown will be unacceptably high. For example, if you risk 10% per trade and lose two in a row, which is very likely, your drawdown is going to be 20%. This is an absurdly large hole to dig your way out. Consider that your capital has decreased by 20%, and the subsequent climb back up needs to be done on lesser capital.

This is why you need to keep your risk per trade low and in line with your strategy's success rate. The best way to manage drawdowns and limit the damage they cause is to put in place risk limits per day, week, and month. Even professional athletes who train to do one thing all the time have bad days, so it's unfair to expect yourself to be at 100% all the time.

These risk limits will take you out of the game when you're playing poorly. A daily risk limit is to prevent you from getting into a spiral of revenge trading. A good limit to stick to when starting is to stop trading if you experience three losses in a row. This is pretty unlikely with options trades to be honest unless you screw up badly, but it's good to have a limit in place from a perspective of the discipline.

Next, aim for a maximum weekly drawdown limit of 5% and a monthly drawdown limit of 6-8%. These are pretty high limits, to be honest, and if you are a directional trader, these limits don't apply to you. Directional traders need to be a lot more conservative than options traders when it comes to risk.

Understand that these are hard stop limits. So, if your account has hit its monthly drawdown level within the first week, you must take a break for a month. Overtrading and a lack of reflection on progress can cause a lot of damage, and a drawdown is simply a reflection of that.

Qualitative Risk

Quantitative metrics aside, your ability to properly manage qualitative things in your life and trading will dictate a lot of your success. Prepare well, and you're likely to see progress. You need to see preparation as your responsibility. I mean, no one else can prepare for you, can they?

CHAPTER 11 AVOIDING BEGINNER MISTAKES AND TIPS

It's very easy for beginners to make mistakes when trading because it's exciting and stressful all at the same time. Let's take a look at some of the mistake's beginners are prone to and think about how to avoid them.

Panicking and exiting early

I did emphasize that you should have a criterion for exiting a position that isn't going in your direction. However, you need to have some flexibility because small moves in the stock translate into big moves in an option. So, you might see your option show up at some $40 in the red. That is an unpleasant prospect but that means that the stock might Have dropped by something like $.60. Now if you think about that you know that it's not uncommon at all for a stock to drop 60 or $.70, and then rebound in the upper direction by a dollar. So, to sell off your option just because there is a small dip like that--unless it's clear that it's part of the downward trend--would be a foolish move. Know that if you think about that, it's not uncommon at all for a stock to drop 60 or $.70, and then rebound in the upper direction by a dollar. So, to sell off your option just because there is a small dip like that unless it's clear that it's part of the downward trend, would be a foolish move. But we can forgive beginners for making a mistake of that nature. It's easy to get panicky when you start seeing your money slip away right before your own eyes.

To deal with these types of situations it's really important to understand a little bit about technical analysis and candlestick charts. These topics are beyond the scope of this book, but you can find information about these topics online, on YouTube, and of course in many books. The point of learning these tools is so that you can look at the chart and estimate where the stock is heading. The tools are far from perfect otherwise everyone would be multimillionaires. However, they are pretty good at giving you an idea that I would call an educated guess. It's better to make an educated guess then it is to panic and sell your option. When I first started, I made the mistake of exiting positions far too early and I would look back later and find that if I had stayed in, I would've made a massive profit. Remember the stock market is always fluctuating a great deal.

Getting Involved in Many Trades at Once

As we've said multiple times spreading yourself too thin is a really bad idea when it comes to trading. The matter what strategy you decide to adopt, my belief is that you should focus on a few different securities and no more. so, what you might sit down and do is pick five stocks that you were really interested in. Hopefully, these are big companies because you want liquidity in the options. Another thing you want is a relatively high share price so that the options have a chance to profit. Know if you are selling options or credit spreads, you definitely want a high share price so that you can earn from the premium. Once you pick out your five companies you should study everything about the companies and know them inside and out. That means looking at their financial statements, knowing when their earnings calls are, and keeping track of things like the volatility, and price to earnings ratio. Then you should study the charts of that company for the past 12 months. Familiarize yourself with the range is that the price has gone through over the past year. None of this is full proof but you were going to be far better off if you were informed rather than simply winging it when trading options.

So, what happens if you do more than five companies? At some point, you're going to be spreading yourself too thin.

If you trade more than five at once it's going to be hard to keep track of the changes in the share prices of companies that you are trading. And to decide whether to get in or out of trades you need to be keeping a close eye on everything. Now some people are maniacs and they are able to divide your attention very well and they like high pressure. If you are a so-called type a personality that likes high pressure, then maybe you can go with as many as you want. But my advice for beginners is that you were going to be better off focusing on a smaller number of companies that you can really study and pay attention to.

Using Too Many Strategies

As I said before one of the first things you should do is sit down and figure out what your goal is with trading options. You don't want to be using a haphazard approach and trying to do this and that and seeing what happens. Instead, decide what your goal is in the best way you want to achieve that goal. Then look at all the different strategies that are available and see what is

The most compatible with your goals. Then apply maybe two or three different strategies at a time. There has to be some flexibility because some situations are going to require one strategy well other situations require a different strategy.

Taking Too Much Risk

If you noticed with the strategies that we examined, there are some trade-offs that have to be made. The trade-offs often involve a trade-off between the amount of profit you can make and the level of risk. People are always greedy I can guarantee that, but one thing that really does is get you into trouble when it comes to trading. You need to be disciplined and methodical. So that means not taking too much risk when it can be avoided. It's better to seek small profits in small bites that can add up rather than trying to hit a home run.

Set It and Forget It

This is a huge mistake the beginners make. They think buying an option is a cool idea, and so they buy an option. But then they don't spend every day studying it and following it. Maybe they hear on the news that the stock drop by five dollars. Then if they go to check their option, they might find that it lost $65 in value. Don't ever take to set it and forget it approach. Every option that you trade, you need to pay attention to in detail every day.

Forgetting About Time Decay

Every day an option is losing extrinsic or time value. But some people leave their options for a long time hoping that the stock is going to move in a favorable direction. Then it never does and they end up losing money when the option expires worthless. So, you have to keep in mind that an option has time decay and that the option is going to lose value because of this. If it's not in the money, that means it's losing value overall.

When Selling Options, Stop Looking at Probabilities

One thing that can also be tempting is to always aim for the highest premium that you can earn when selling a credit spread. That is a bad strategy. Even though you might get a large credit, you might also put yourself in a high risk of assignment. The goal should be to set up trades that have a high probability of success. Would you rather have a trade that might make $200 but it has a 65% chance of failure, or would you rather have a trade that made $75 and had a 95% chance of success? I think it's the latter that would appeal to most people. The thing is the $75 is just one trade. You can do 10 or 20 of those trades.

Not Paying Attention to Volatility

Every time you look up an option, I advise you to look at the implied volatility. This is actually an estimate of the future volatility of the stock that underlies the option. If the implied volatility is high that means higher option prices generally speaking. If you're selling options, you are going to want to sell options where the implied volatility is higher.

Not Having a Training Plan

Besides setting general goals, you should have a trading plan in place. The first part of your training plan would be to establish how much money you're willing to risk on every trade. Another thing to look at is what strategy are you going to use to determine which trades to enter? For example, you might just do it on a whim when it seems like the stock is going up. In fact, that's how most people view the markets. but you could take a different approach instead of doing that what you could do is have a technical analysis-based reason to enter a trade. For example, if the stock price has been dropping but then there's a golden cross which means that a short period moving average has crossed over on top of the lawn. Moving average, this is a good sign that you should enter a trade. So, you could start your week picking out the stocks that you're interested in for that week. I advise working with a small number of stocks at any given time, so you could pick three such as Facebook, Lucky Martin, and Amazon. Then what you do is you studied the charts and wait for the right moment to enter the trade.

Not Giving Enough Time or Even Thinking About Time

It's important to think about the expiration date that you pick when trading options. There is always a possibility that an option it's going down is going to rebound later on if there is a long time until the expiration. So, if there was only three days left for an option, and it was losing money, that is a trade that I would definitely say cut your losses. But if there are three weeks left, panicking every time the option goes down in value is a really bad idea. Instead, you need to let it sit there and wait until the right moment to sell it. Even if that means only going so far is breaking even so you can get out of the trade without losing money. But the time left expiration is a very important factor in deciding how to handle that situation.

CONCLUSION

Thank you for making it to the end. Whatever your reasons for trading options, you might have questions about how to do it effectively. That's why we have this Options Trading Crash Course for Beginners.

The primary purpose of trading options is to make money by essentially buying an option contract so that you can sell it before the expiration date. There are two types of options contracts: call and put. You can also buy a combination of calls and puts, known as a synthetic option. These contracts are bought for two reasons: to gain exposure to an asset, and to profit from a shift in the underlying asset's value as time passes.

Options have grown in popularity because they offer investors with potential high profits without investment risk. However, like any investment, there are risks associated with options. When you buy an option, you are giving up an opportunity to make money, but if you don't buy an option at all, then you're taking on nothing but risk.

If volatility increases or decreases, then the price of an underlying asset could move in either direction very differently than anticipated.

There are tremendous benefits to trading options. We understand the challenges investors face when trading options. That is why with the help of this book and the other of the series you will know what you need in order to make sure you can truly make an informed decision about your options strategy and trade.

Options Trading can be very profitable if you know what you are doing.

Trading options is a very simple process. If you want to buy it, then look for a stock that is about to go up and buy it with the option in order to profit sometime in the future. If the stock goes up the option gives you more profit over time so the total profit would be higher than if you had only bought the stock.

On the other hand, if you want to sell the option, then look for a stock that is about to go down and sell it with the option in order to profit sometime in the future. If the stock goes down, then your gain will be larger than if you had only sold the stock without this option.

If you're new to options trading or are unsure about how to best invest your money, we're here to assist. This book is always available to answer any questions you may have.

In case, however, you feel that this manual is not enough and you want to dive deeper into the world of Options Trading, learn the winning strategies, secrets and tools, we invite you to discover the other manuals in the series:

OPTIONS TRADING CRASH COURSE: FUNDAMENTALS *Everything you need to know before you start investing like a real trader*

OPTIONS TRADING CRASH COURSE: SWING TRADING DAY TRADING AND BEST STRATEGIES *The best strategies to operate in the market in the most profitable way*

OPTIONS TRADING CRASH COURSE: ADVANCED OPTIONS TRADING TOOLS *A simple* *but effective guide to operate in the market in a smart and conscious way*

www.ingramcontent.com/pod-product-compliance
Lightning Source LLC
Chambersburg PA
CBHW050451190326
41458CB00005B/1241

* 9 7 8 1 9 1 4 5 9 9 7 4 3 *